W9-BBS-601

Christian A. Schwarz

The Threefold Art of Experiencing God

The Liberating Power of a Trinitarian Faith

ChurchSmart
RESOURCES

This booklet provides insight into the background of an approach to church growth which has become known as "natural church development." Working material relating to the theory and practice of natural church development will be available in about 30 languages by the year 2000. Titles and ordering information can be found on the internet at:

http://www.CundP.de/international

Published by ChurchSmart Resources
Carol Stream, IL 60188

For a free catalog of our resources call 1-800-253-4276

© 1999 Christian A. Schwarz

© U.S.A. edition: ChurchSmart Resources, Carol Stream, IL 60188

Original title: Die dreifache Kunst Gott zu erleben
Published 1999 by C & P Verlag, Emmelsbüll, Germany

Cover design: Heidenreich Kommunikationsdesign
Printing: M.C.E. HOREB, Viladecavalls (Barcelona), Spain
Printed in Spain

All Rights Reserved
ISBN 1-889638-14-5

The Threefold Art of Experiencing God

Notice:

Since mere words cannot adequately communicate the mystery of the divine Trinity, this booklet has been developed around the many diagrams—quite the opposite of what one would normally expect in a book. The main concepts are conveyed through the diagrams; the words simply expound on what has been presented graphically.

It is possible to approach the topic by first studying only the diagrams (together with the captions), and only then reading the complete booklet. It is also conceivable—and even desirable—that you attach to the diagrams your own comments describing your personal situation or that of your church. Finally, you could deal with this booklet by first completely dispensing with the written explanations and restricting yourself to approaching the views of our relationship to God, as conveyed through the illustrations, in a purely meditative way.

Why I Am Writing About the Trinity

> *"The God whom we can experience in a threefold way— that is the most practical theological topic I know."*

The Trinity: For most Christians this is one of the most sophisticated, difficult, and abstract topics of theology. If people have dealt with this subject at all, then it's certainly not been in connection with practical issues such as "church development" or "personal spiritual growth." Pushing the doctrine of the Trinity away from life into the scholar's study has had terrible consequences. In my opinion, the widespread lack of understanding of the God who reveals himself in a threefold way, is the main reason for the shocking paralysis of vast sectors of Christianity. It also explains why we Christians have difficulty in dealing with the challenges confronting us in the new millennium.

The confession of God as Father, Son and Holy Spirit is what distinguishes Christianity from all religions. If it is the specific feature of the Christian faith, it should also be the premise for our reflection on the practical side of church life. We should not expect to solve the pressing problems of our churches by methodical gimmicks, but rather by reconsidering this center. In my seminars, I have made the same discovery again and again: A new understanding of the Trinity not only leads us toward a new view of God, it also guides to new experiences with God. It leads to a deeper recognition of our strengths, our limitations, our images of adversaries, our dreams, and our fears. In an amazingly simple way it explains the conflicts which so often paralyze Christianity, and can become a creative key in directing the energy hidden beneath such conflicts toward a constructive process of change.

Natural church development

My starting point is not an abstract Christian ideal, but rather empirical Christianity. In the last few years, my ministry with the Institute for Natural Church Development has brought me into contact with Christian churches on all six continents. I have dealt with extremely different groups—evangelicals, charismatics, liberals—but the problems we all struggle with are similar in nature. My purpose in all my writing and teaching is not to pursue theology for the sake of theology, but rather to contribute to a solution of these problems.

Between 1994 and 1996, we carried the empirical approach to a certain extreme, when we conducted a comprehensive research project of the causes of church growth. Up to now, about 5,000 churches in more than 50 countries have participated in this study. I have presented the most important conclusions from this research in the book *Natural Church Development*. The main insight: If we concentrate on the "roots" (i.e. the quality of the church), then the "fruit" (i.e. the quantity) will grow automatically. The study was an attempt to take a look under the surface (see diagram below). We have, to put it metaphorically, dug around in the "dirt," which cannot be studied as long as we remain on the surface. In this booklet I would like to invite you to reverse our focal point and join me in gazing "heavenwards." The synopsis of both perspectives—from "below" and from "above"—will help us to better understand the approach of creation theology which provides the base for natural church development.

The origin of this booklet

This booklet has a somewhat crazy history. At one of my seminars, I wanted to take a whole day to work with the group on the trinitarian approach, but the organizers refused: "Far too theoretical!" Finally they allowed me to use three quarters of an hour for the topic, but requested that in the same amount of time I also deal with the main insights from my book *Paradigm Shift in the Church* (a book of about 300 pages and more than 600 footnotes). At first I protested against the curtailment; but finally I agreed.

I invested several weeks in the preparation of these forty-five minutes. What I experienced from the participants, was an almost explosive "aha effect," which I have encountered whenever I have conveyed these thoughts in short-form. This is the main reason why I am trying in this booklet to present the most complex topic of theology in a mere 32 pages.

Many believers consider the trinitarian creed of Christianity to be a "dry formula." As a matter of fact, I agree with this view. But we shouldn't forget that the concept of nuclear fission has been captured in a "dry formula" as well. What the formula contains and what it effects are crucial. The classical trinitarian formulas might appear dry, strange, and even irrelevant. The God who can be experienced in a threefold way—that is the most practical theological topic I know. When we set it free from the abstractions of theological formulas, its explosive power can revolutionize both our personal lives and our churches.

The creation-oriented approach which is the foundation of natural church development: If the roots are healthy, the fruit will grow "automatically."

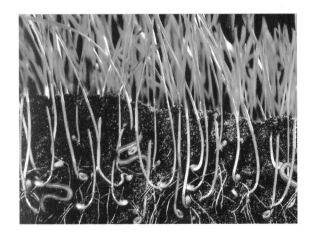

5

1 Believing Is Experiencing

"The point is not whether we believe in the Trinity, but rather that we believe in a trinitarian way."

The center of the Christian faith is not man, nor the church, but God. This one God is perceived by people in different ways. Just as light that falls through a prism fans out into a wide spectrum of various colors, human beings perceive the one God in various ways (see diagram on the right).

It is essential to the Christian view of God that God is not simply reduced to a "notion" or a "power." The biblical understanding is that God is a person. If God were merely a philosophical category, the most suitable way to get to know him would be intellectual reflection. But if God is a person, the only possible way of knowledge suitable to the object of our search is a personal encounter with this person. Who would suggest to "know" somebody if one had never met him, had never communicated with him, and had no personal relationship with him? When I advocate "experience" as a way to get knowledge about God, it has nothing to do with mystical, esoteric teaching. Without the dimension of experience it is absolutely impossible to comprehend the Christian faith. God cannot be found "per se," but only in a relationship "to us."

What does it mean "to get to know God"?

It is interesting that in the Old Testament the same word which is used for "to know" *(jada')* is also used for "sexual intercourse." Knowing God, in the biblical sense, is comparable to the holistic, sensual and pleasurable encounter between man and woman. While the theology professor who is poring over his books is hardly a good model for "knowledge" in the biblical sense, the sexual relationship between two people certainly is. The fact that some Christians find such statements "offensive" only indicates how far removed our understanding of God is from that of the Bible.

Faith without experiences

In the last few years I have had to acquire at least a basic understanding of many languages in the most economical way. For this reason I primarily have used dictionaries which are based on the results of so-called "language frequency research." These dictionaries, arranged under topic headings, contain only those words which have been proven through an analysis of newspapers, conversations, etc. to actually be used in everyday language.

Of course, the section "religion" or "faith" was particularly interesting to me. In none of the above mentioned dictionaries was I able to find terms such as "experience," "encounter," or "desire" (the last keyword was listed under the heading "sexuality"). But in almost all of them, under the heading "religion," I could only find terms such

6

God

as "priest," "cemetery," and "Gothic." In other words, key Christian categories such as experience, encounter and desire—terms without which the Christian faith ceases to exist!—are seen as dispensable; priest, cemetery and Gothic are not. That this is not the opinion of opponents of the Christian faith, but rather the result of research of the words actually used in the field of religion, speaks more of the condition of empirical Christianity than most of us would like to admit.

The Trinity as a category of experience

Our three-colored diagram would be misunderstood if it was simply interpreted to mean that people perceive God differently. God revealed himself in three different ways. What we now call the "doctrine of the Trinity" was originally nothing more than a category of experience. The early Christians recognized God as Creator, experienced Christ as God through prayer, and sensed the power of the Holy Spirit in their lives. In other words: they *experienced* God in a threefold manner—and as a result they *thought* about the Trinity. The same holds true today. The crucial point is not that we believe in the Trinity, but rather that we believe in a trinitarian way; in other words, that we experience God in a threefold manner.

Three Ways of Experiencing God

"In all three revelations we encounter the one God, but each time we encounter him in a different way."

The threefold revelation of God is normally referred to by the terms "Father," "Son," and "Holy Spirit." I have tried to express the same in the diagram, but deliberately have chosen terms which do not refer to the relationship these three entities have *to each other,* but to the relationship God has *to us.* In this booklet I would like to keep strictly to this given: since the God of the Bible can only be appropriately understood in his relationship "to us," I will unfold my thoughts exclusively within this relational framework and choose the terminology accordingly.

It is characteristic of all three revelations that God not only reveals "something" of himself, but also his own nature. This applies to the "creation revelation" (the green segment of the diagram), as well as to the "salvation revelation" (the red segment), and to the "personal revelation" (the blue segment). It is important for our topic that we understand the specific character of each of these three revelations.

The "creation revelation"

God revealed himself as Creator by leaving the marks of his handwriting on creation (Ps. 19:2; Rom. 1:19f). One does not have to be a Christian in order to encounter this type of revelation **(green segment)**. Whether I am a Muslim, Buddhist, atheist or Christian—when I turn to creation I can sense the fingerprints of the Creator. This type of revelation is international, interdenominational—in fact interreligious (note that these statements are describing the creation revelation, not the salvation revelation or the personal revelation!). Thus it is obvious that the creation revelation can be understood differently and also can be misunderstood. On the basis of this form of revelation alone nobody will come to the realization that the Creator is the Father of Jesus Christ.

The "salvation revelation"

The salvation revelation **(red segment)** has a different character. Jesus is the one in whom we definitely see God for who he really is (John 14:9). In Christ, God became man, in him "all the fullness of the Deity lives in bodily form" (Col. 2:9). He is the one who reconciles us with God (2 Cor. 5:19). According to the New Testament, our relationship to Jesus Christ determines our salvation or damnation (Acts 4:12). Through him we receive "eternal life" (Rom. 6:23).

The "personal revelation"

I refer to the personal revelation **(blue segment)** as the occasion where what God did for us objectively in Christ becomes a subjective reality. Through the Holy Spirit, the "Christ for us" becomes the

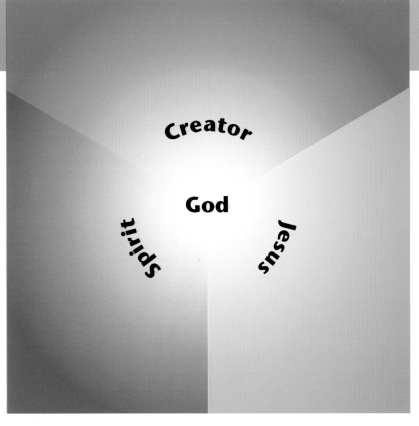

Creator

God

Spirit

Jesus

God is not only perceived by humans in different ways, but he has also revealed himself to us in various ways: creation revelation (green segment), salvation revelation (red segment), and personal revelation (blue segment).

"Christ in us" (Gal. 2:20, 4:19, Col. 1:27). Through the Holy Spirit, God pours his love into our hearts (Rom. 5:5). Through him, God's Spirit enters into a relationship with our spirit. Thus a human being can literally become "the temple of the Holy Spirit" (1 Cor. 6:19). The revelation of the Holy Spirit is the revelation in our hearts. It happens, for example, when a person becomes a Christian (1 Cor. 12:3). If this personal appropriation does not take place, the revelation of God has not achieved its goal.

God's revelations always aim at establishing a relationship. In all three revelations we encounter the one God, but each time we encounter him in a different way. His threefold communication with us, which should correspond with a threefold response on our part, is fundamental to the nature of God as revealed to us in the Bible. Whenever just one of the three dimensions is neglected, we have an incomplete experience of God. We will come to see that most problems with which we struggle in the everyday life of our churches are, in the final analysis, based on an incomplete understanding of the threefold revelation of God.

Revelation = enablement of a relationship

The Mystery of the Trinity

"God's reality is revealed to us only in his actions."

Nobody can recognize the nature of radium as long as he or she does not understand its effect, radioactivity. In a similar way, nobody will be able to comprehend the nature of God as long as he or she does not understand his deeds. The reality of God is revealed to us only in his actions.

On these two pages I have tried to link up the threefold revelation of God with various aspects of God's work. On the left-hand side, I have presented consequences which arise out of the threefold revelation as described in the last chapter. The right-hand side deals with consequences which extend far beyond the Trinity, but in view of God's communication with us, resemble a similar inner structure.

Three works

The *first picture* indicates the most immediate consequence of the threefold revelation of God: the green segment is designated for "creation," the red segment for "salvation," the blue segment for "sanctification." In all three cases, it is the same God (white circle) who does this work. At the same time these three works of God can be related to one of the three forms of revelation.

Three manners of being

The *second picture* expresses three different "places" where God meets us: The eternal God, whom we know is "above us" (green segment), comes through the incarnation of Jesus Christ "among us" (red segment), and at the same time produces the knowledge of his presence "within us" (blue segment). The one God can be encountered at all of these three places.

Three forms of address

The *third picture* sketches three practical consequences for our life. The three revelations of God embody the *appeal* ("You shall!", green segment), the *invitation* ("You may!", red segment), and the

Three works

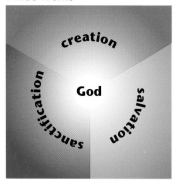

Three manners of being

Three forms of address

empowerment ("You can!", blue segment). Only those who have come to know God in all three ways will be able to serve God according to his plan.

The *fourth picture* makes clear that this threefold communication of God with us humans is already characteristic of the Old Testament. Israel first experienced God as the God of his people (i.e. in history, red segment), and then inquired in what respect he is also the God of the world or nature (green segment), as well as the God of the individual (blue segment). Already here we have one of the roots of the later doctrine of the Trinity, which guides us to believing in the same God in history, nature, and existence.

Three levels of reality

The *fifth picture* describes three great covenants of God, which correspond with the three levels of reality just described: the Noah covenant (green segment) as an expression of God's power over nature, the Sinai covenant (red segment) as an expression of God's power over history, and finally the Abraham covenant (blue segment) as a document for the fact that God also has promises for individuals who believe.

Three covenants

The *sixth picture*, finally, relates the same threeness to an area which has special significance in light of our topic. Here we are dealing with three sources from which we can gain knowledge: science (green segment), the Bible (red segment), and experience (blue segment). It should be clear that these three sources are not given the same rank (not every source produces a valid knowledge of God), and yet we can encounter the fingerprints of God in each area.

Three sources of knowledge

Three levels of reality

Three covenants

Three sources of knowledge

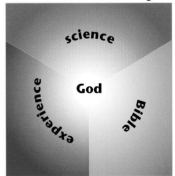

4 A Christian Pantheon of Gods?

"Once we have put the three persons next to each other, almost like 'three gods,' we are not far away from allowing people to select their 'favorite god' out of this pantheon."

So far the whole matter does not appear to be very complicated: there are three ways to encounter God—but we are always dealing with the same God. As long as we limit ourselves by understanding the Trinity as a category of experience, we are not confronted by insurmountable intellectual problems. God has revealed himself in a threefold way, and he has always revealed himself as the one, complete, perfect, undivided God.

But problems do occur as soon as we abstract the Trinity from the dimension of experience and make it a pure category of thinking. Instead of meditating on the relationship that *we humans* have to the one God (or the relationship God has to us), one mentally puts the "three persons of the Godhood" (as the classical terminology called it) next to each other and asks oneself what kind of relationship these three persons have *to each other*.

This was the starting point of intense discussions which shook the church in the fourth century AD and finally led to the official doctrine of the Trinity. The church was looking for verbal formulas which expressed not only the "unity of God," but also the "diversity of the three persons." But which terms were suitable for this purpose? There were bitter struggles about this question. The Roman Emperor Constantine, who needed the church (which had up to then been persecuted by the state) within the framework of his power politics, was looking for ways to end this dispute. He invited, at public expense, the bishops and theologians to a large council in Nicea and spared no effort—including his own theological contributions—in finding formulas with which all opposing parties could identify, so that they would finally calm down.

The classical doctrine of the Trinity

From these discussions arose the classical doctrine of the Trinity, which applies to this day: God is understood as "one substance," but "three persons" *(una substantia, tres personae)*. What can be said about this formula in the light of what has become clear to us about the Trinity so far? At least three things:

1. This formula was supposed to express the same concept I have tried to present in this booklet with the aid of the three-colored diagram. But if we try to grasp this truth exclusively by means of language—and Latin or Greek at that—it becomes a very difficult undertaking. If the discussions about the Trinity over the centuries have proven anything at all, it is that this question cannot be tackled through words alone.

2. It shows us how problematic it is to isolate the Trinity from the relational aspect—almost as if we were observing a lifeless object under the microscope. Thus in the following debates it became unavoidable to deal more and more with the inter-trinitarian relationships (as if they were *our* problems!). The less the Trinity is experienced existentially, the more the danger arises that it will become the object of contention in philosophical speculation.

3. The terminology used may have been the best available at the time. However, when we apply our *present* understanding of "person" to the formula that was developed at that time, immense confusion arises. It is simply impossible to think of "three persons" as anything else but "tri-theistic," regardless of how much one protests against this interpretation. In the same way, our present conception of substance, when applied to God, leads us to an understanding which does not have much in common with the view of God presented in Scripture.

Do we have to believe in the doctrine of the Trinity?

At the time of the Nicean council, there were almost no meaningful alternatives to the terms used. But today we can express the same truth differently. We do not have to believe in the (Nicean) doctrine of the Trinity; but rather we should strive to encounter the God who has revealed himself in a threefold manner, holistically. If our resources—whether they be theological formulas or visual aids or meditation in solitude—help us to discover the fullness of God, they have fulfilled their purpose.

The consequences

It can be shown that the formulas which were found—even though they were meant to achieve the opposite—contributed in their historical effect toward a segmentation of God. Of course, God has not really been segmented, but what has been segmented is the possibility of experiencing God in a holistic way. Once we have put the three divine persons next to each other almost like "three gods" at least psychologically (theologically this possibility was, of course, rejected), then we are not far from giving each Christian the option to choose his or her own "favorite God" out of this Christian pantheon. This division of God corresponds to a segmentation among Christians, which is in turn the reason for numerous self-made blockages which dominate the Christian church up to this day.

5   A Segmented God

"Each of the three groups can be considered as an advocate for one of the three ways in which God reveals himself."

Once our view of God has been reduced to one of the three ways in which God reveals himself (expressed in the categories of the diagram: one of the three colors), we have also reduced our possibilities of experiencing God. This is exactly the tragedy which we Christians are confronted with today. In worldwide Christianity there are three main groups who, positively seen, can be considered as advocates for one of the three ways in which God has revealed himself: the "liberals" as advocates for the creation revelation, the "evangelicals" as advocates for the salvation revelation, the "charismatics" as advocates for the personal revelation.

Depending on which group we belong to, we will attach more negative or positive associations with the above mentioned terms. "Liberals," for example, find it hard to understand why some Christians consider this term an abusive word. The same holds true for "evangelicals" or "charismatics" in view of their respective names.

The meaning of the three terms

When we critically examine the three groups, we should not forget that each of the three terms outlines central concerns of the biblical message. The term "liberal" is based on the Latin word *liber,* which means free and reminds us of the biblical theme of liberation. The word "evangelical" stems from gospel *(euaggelion),* the good news, and is one of the most beautiful words which Christianity has produced. Finally, the word "charismatic" can be traced back to the Greek word *charis,* which simply means "grace." Freedom, gospel, grace—who would care to doubt that all three terms are dealing with central biblical themes?

Before we critically examine the divisions of the three groups and ask how these divisions can be overcome, it seems to me to be very important to recognize the justified concerns of each group.

The "liberals"

Since the "liberals" **(green segment)** are advocates for the creation revelation, it is no coincidence that they concentrate on themes such as preservation of creation, peace, and justice. They put a strong emphasis on the political dimension of the Christian faith as well as themes like sensuality, art, liturgy, and science.

The "evangelicals"

The "evangelicals" **(red segment)** as advocates for the salvation revelation emphasize the necessity of a personal relationship to Jesus. It is no coincidence that they stress the absolute claim of Jesus. For evangelicals the topic of "evangelism" is of utmost importance: people who would be lost without Christ, shall be saved.

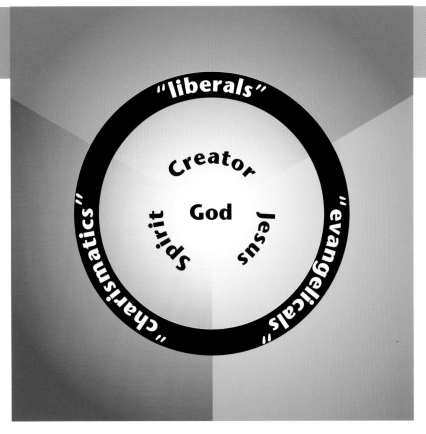

The three main groups which shape Christianity and very often are in conflict with each other: liberals, evangelicals, and charismatics. Positively seen, each of these groups can be considered an advocate for one of the three ways in which God reveals himself.

The "charismatics" **(blue segment)** are advocates for the personal revelation. For them it is important to experience the reality of the power of the Holy Spirit—not only as an intellectual category, but rather as a life-changing power in daily life. It is certainly not the case that non-charismatics have completely excluded the "Holy Spirit," but for charismatics this topic is absolutely central. That explains why they are so interested in the gifts and manifestations of the Spirit.

The "charismatics"

Problems between the three groups always arise when one of the three concerns—regardless which one!—is isolated from the others and played off against them. But this is exactly what usually happens. Once God has been segmented into three persons, each group can choose their own "favorite god": the liberals choose the Creator, the evangelicals Jesus, and the charismatics the Holy Spirit. The more these three concerns are isolated from one another, the more intense the conflict between these three groups gets.

The other side of the coin

6 How Heresies Develop

"Either the boundary between truth and error runs between the colored segments, or between the 'inside' and the 'outside.'"

The diagram indicates what can occur if one of the three concerns is isolated from the other two. All three terms outside the circle ("syncretism," "dogmatism," and "spiritualism") designate heresies, and each is placed next to the group which is particularly susceptible to it.

Different interpretations are possible depending on whether we observe the color outside or inside the circle. The green color can, on the one hand, be the green in nature (inside the circle), but it can also be the green of fundamentalist eco-ideologists (outside the circle). The red can symbolize the blood of Jesus Christ (inside), but it can also be seen as the red of a "stop sign" (outside). The blue can symbolize wind (inside)—in Hebrew as well as Greek the same word is used for "wind" and "spirit"—but it can also refer to the ocean, where everything is in a state of flux and nothing has clear contours (outside).

The danger of syncretism

Syncretism **(the green segment)** means mixture of religions. This danger, to which liberals are especially vulnerable, has its roots in the creation revelation, which by its very nature is interreligious. In order to share the concerns which liberals have put (for good biblical reasons) on their banners, one does not have to be a Christian. Principles of creation apply to all people—Christians and non-Christians alike—since all people have been created by God. Syncretism attempts to become emancipated from the absolute claims of Jesus (red segment) and the dimension of the Holy Spirit (blue segment).

The danger of dogmatism

The specific danger for evangelicals is dogmatism **(red segment)**: the correct doctrine of Jesus finally becomes more important than the personal relationship to him. This is the very danger evangelicals originally fought against. The more extreme the influence of dogmatism is (and the more the red part is isolated from the other two), the more the "correct doctrine" will take the place of a living faith. This can be studied by looking at the development of the Pietistic movement. Originally it had been—together with the Enlightenment—a protest movement against dead orthodoxy. But some parts of the Pietistic movement became gradually "orthodox" themselves, i.e. all the distinctives of orthodoxy became evident in its own groups.

The danger of spiritualism

The specific danger for charismatics is spiritualism **(blue segment)**: spiritual experiences become more important than the standards of Scripture (red segment). Spiritualistic tendencies often become evi-

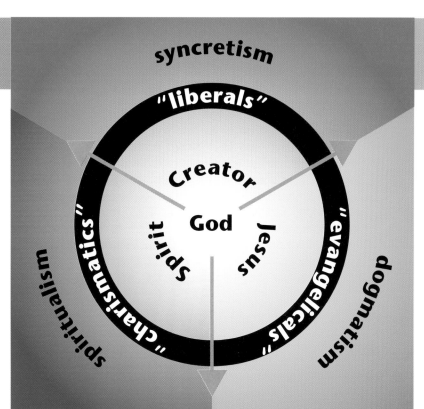

Whenever one of the three segments is isolated from the other two, heresies develop, which are indicated outside the circle. The main danger for the liberals is syncretism, for the evangelicals it is dogmatism, and for the charismatics it is spiritualism.

dent in hostile ("anti-green") attitudes toward creation. Not every "charismatic" tends toward spiritualism, only those who isolate the blue segment and play it off against the other two.

We now have two possibilities of interpretation. Either we take each color—regardless whether inside or outside the circle—as a complete whole and keep the boundary between truth and error identical with the boundary between the individual colors. For example, "all the red, regardless if a living faith in Jesus or dogmatism, is right; all the green, regardless whether biblically oriented or syncretistic, is wrong."

Second possibility: The boundary between truth and error is not marked by the colors but rather by the black circle which encompasses the center. All three light color tones inside the circle represent the biblical position; all three dark colors outside the circle indicate heresies. Whoever begins psychologically with "three different gods," will not be able to avoid the first interpretation; but whoever begins with the one God who has revealed himself in three ways, will give preference to the second interpretation. Their goal will be to move closer and closer to the center of the circle to unite all three concerns within their own persons.

Two types of interpretation

17

Self-Assessment: Which "Colors" Do You Reflect?

"Note that the yellow circle always moves as a complete whole."

It is helpful for each one of us to discover to which of the three segments we lean. There are four "pure" positions, which are relatively seldom held: the three heresies of syncretism, dogmatism, and spiritualism, as well as the ideal of a perfect integration of all three colors (see diagram at above right). Mixed forms (see diagrams below) and, especially, "coalitions" (see diagrams on bottom right) are much more common. All of these positions actually reflect aspects of each of the others—they just place a different emphasis on each. Examine each of the six positions and ask yourself about your own tendencies. It is meaningful to conduct this self-analysis in three areas:

a. Where am I *rationally,* i.e. in view of my thinking?

b. Where am I *emotionally,* i.e. in view of my heart?

c. Where am I *socially,* i.e. in view of my network of relationships?

Green: Liberals

Strengths: social involvement, science

Weakness: few shared parts with the blue and red segment

Opponent: dogmatism and spiritualism

More helpful boundary would be: syncretism

Areas of spiritual growth: red and blue segments

Red: Evangelicals

Strengths: evangelism, Bible

Weakness: few shared parts with green and blue segments

Opponent: syncretism, spiritualism

More helpful boundary would be: dogmatism

Areas for spiritual growth: green and blue segments

Blue: Charismatics

Strengths: spirituality, personal experience

Weakness: few shared parts with green and red segments

Opponent: dogmatism, syncretism

More helpful boundary would be: spiritualism

Areas of spiritual growth: red and green segments

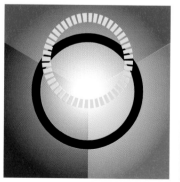

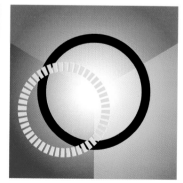

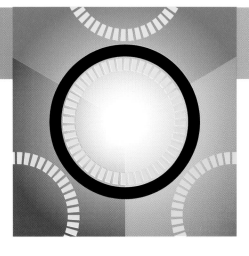

The responses can be very different for each area. As you interpret the results, remember that as a rule the yellow circle moves as a whole. As it is pushed toward the center, it automatically leaves the area of "heresy" outside of

The four positions in their pure forms. While the circle in the middle depicts the ideal, the three outer circles depict "heresies."

the black circle. The positive movement in the direction of the center is usually more conducive than the active battle against heresy. With the description of each individual position I have suggested areas of growth, and identified the heresies which can serve as boundaries. These boundaries alert us to our specific dangers in our spiritual development.

Red-green: liberal-evangelical coalition

Strength: Jesus-piety connected with involvement in society

Weakness: blue segment fades out, compromises within red and green segment

Opponent: charismatics

Areas for spiritual growth: pneumatology

Red-blue: evangelical-charismatic coalition

Strengths: biblical clarity connected with spiritual experience

Weakness: green segment fades out, compromises in red and blue segments

Opponent: liberals

Areas for spiritual growth: creation theology

Blue-green: charismatic-liberal coalition

Strength: intellectual open-mindedness connected with spirituality

Weakness: red segment fades out, compromises in green and blue segments

Opponent: evangelicals

Areas of spiritual growth: Christology

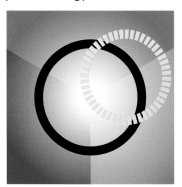 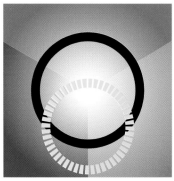 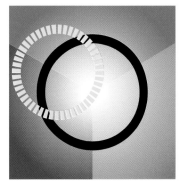

8   Learning from God's Creation

"The law of polarity says that for every pole there is a counter pole."

What we have termed "natural church development" is a decidedly "trinitarian approach" to church growth, i.e. it tries to include all three colors in our diagram, including the green segment. For instance, the "biotic principles" of natural church development stem from neither Christology (red segment) nor pneumatology (blue segment), but rather from God's revelation in creation.

This explains why some groups—especially those we have described with the terms "dogmatism" and "spiritualism"—view this approach somewhat skeptically. This skepticism, however, can also spill over to "evangelicals" or "charismatics." Since neither has adequately integrated the "green position" into their view of God and experience, they will not be able to get rid of the suspicion that this approach is spiritually dubious.

Since some of the basic principles of natural church development correspond to the green segment, we can understand the skepticism which it encounters in some groups.

It is remarkable how frequently Jesus, whenever he spoke about the kingdom of God and its dynamics, referred to the "green segment" (i.e. creation revelation). His message, presented in various ways, is, "If you want to know which principles apply to the kingdom of God, learn from the creation of my Heavenly Father." The best example for this is Matthew 6:28, where Jesus admonishes us to carefully study the growth mechanisms of the "lilies on the field." This study of the organic laws, mind you, is no "Bible study." It is rather a study of God's creation.

If we accept this approach, we will encounter again and again the law of polarity, which runs through all of God's creation. A good example of this is the human brain, where the left and right side of the brain have different functions. Whereas isolation from each other would result in death, their healthy cooperation provides the secret to human creativity. Or consider the different poles in electricity, in magnetism, and in the relationship of the two sexes.

The law of polarity says that for every pole there is a counter pole. Both are in creative tension toward each other. This bipolarity releases a stream of energy which has—as best exemplified by the attraction between

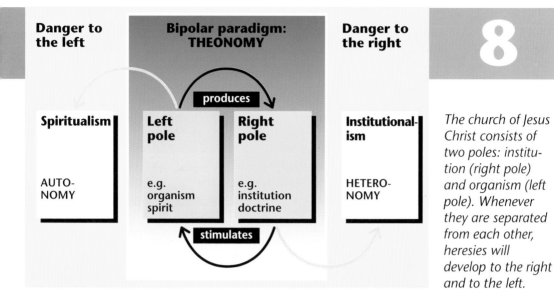

Danger to the left	Bipolar paradigm: THEONOMY	Danger to the right	**8**

produces

Spiritualism	Left pole	Right pole	Institutional-ism
AUTO-NOMY	e.g. organism spirit	e.g. institution doctrine	HETERO-NOMY

stimulates

The church of Jesus Christ consists of two poles: institution (right pole) and organism (left pole). Whenever they are separated from each other, heresies will develop to the right and to the left.

the male and female poles—direct consequences on reproduction of life itself. Without polarity, no life!

Bipolarity in the church

In my book *Paradigm Shift in the Church,* I have dealt comprehensively with the reason why this bipolarity is fundamental to the church of Jesus Christ. The diagram above summarizes these facts in a condensed form. The church consists of an organic (left) as well as an organizational pole (right). While the organic pole, for example, can be related to the term "spirit," the organizational pole is characterized by terms such as "doctrine." The secret of healthy churches is that both poles can harmoniously coexist. If they are separated, the dangers described in the graphs will develop to the left and to the right.

Dangers to the right and to the left

If the right (institutional) pole is isolated, the danger of institutionalism emerges. I use this term to describe a whole paradigm of thinking which is based on a heteronomic structure. Heteronomy occurs when institutions, doctrines, and orders take the place which only God deserves.

On the other hand, if the left (spiritual) pole is isolated from its institutional, doctrinal counterpart, the danger of spiritualism emerges, which is fed on the human drive for *autonomy* (self-determination). Here, in the final analysis, human beings with their subjective feelings put themselves in the place of God.

The bipolar paradigm—characterized by the interrelationship of both poles in the center—is no mixture of the mentioned heresies, but rather an alternative which can help to overcome both dangers. I have chosen the term "theonomy" for this position: here God has the place which only he is entitled to.

"Heteronomy as well as autonomy are, according to the Bible, sin."

Behind both "false paradigms"—autonomy as well as heterono-my—questionable views of God are hidden, as indicated in the diagram on page 29 (where I have combined the bipolar paradigm with our trinitarian graph).

Characteristic of the heteronomic paradigm is its tendency to objec-tivism. Faith is primarily understood as believing certain doctrines, keeping of moral standards, membership in a specific institution. Those who tend toward this view see, for example, the recitation of the Christian creed (which has exclusively to do with the proclama-tion of facts that should be believed) almost as "prayer."

Characteristics of a heteronomic understanding of faith

Psychologically, this system of thinking is founded on a need for se-curity. Since such a theology meets the needs of many people, rep-resentatives of this approach can expect a certain number of follow-ers even in our day. Heteronomists are people for whom order equals happiness. They long for someone who will do their thinking and prescribe to them in every detail what is right and what is wrong.

The danger to the right: the institu-tional pole is seen as an absolute.

For representatives of this paradigm, the Bible is nothing more than a book of laws. In the final analysis, the heteronomic understanding of faith is possible without the Holy Spirit, without love, without surprises. Here the law has replaced God—and at the same time it has replaced life.

This approach to faith can lead to many false assumptions:

• "Celebrate the worship service in a given form, and the Holy Spirit will auto-matically be present."

• "Believe in the infallibili-ty of the Bible, and God's Word will automatically speak to you."

• "Believe certain dogmas, and you will automatically be a Christian."

• "Use a certain church growth program, and your church will automatically blossom and grow."

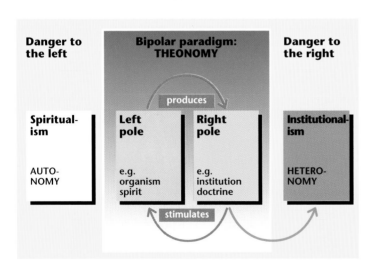

Danger to the left	Bipolar paradigm: THEONOMY		Danger to the right
	produces		
Spiritual-ism	**Left pole**	**Right pole**	**Institutional-ism**
AUTO-NOMY	e.g. organism spirit	e.g. institution doctrine	HETERO-NOMY
	stimulates		

The "autonomous paradigm" (danger to the left) refers to a subjective countermovement. Representatives of this approach have problems not only with the symptoms of institutionalism; they are against all forms of institutions—as a matter of principle. In some cases this anti-institutional affect can grow into a general hostility toward the church; others come to terms with the unavoidability of the institution. They do not fight against it, but consider it spiritually meaningless.

Characteristics of an autonomous understanding of faith

Whereas the psychological motive of those who embrace the heteronomic paradigm is a search for security, those with an autonomous understanding of faith desire absolute independence, freedom, and spontaneity. If heteronomy idolizes the law, representatives of the autonomous paradigm idolize themselves. The doctrinal element can even be seen as an enemy that has to be attacked.

While the heteronomic model of faith tends toward rationalism (only what can be explained rationally is "true"), representatives of spiritualism tend to grant the irrational a higher spiritual value than things that can be explained. They do not understand that rationality (mind you: not rationalism!) is a gift of God. For them—logically as a result of their thought paradigm—both terms are synonyms.

While quite different, both heteronomy and autonomy lead to sin. While those with a security mentality tend to ignore the nature of faith, those who favor autonomy often display a self-glorifying emancipation from God's orders.

The danger to the left: the spiritual pole is seen as an absolute.

Whereas in the context of the bipolar paradigm, both order (right pole) and spontaneity (left pole) are needed, the false paradigms play these poles against each other.

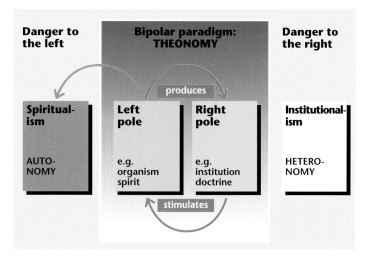

"The debate has been continuing for 2000 years —without any significant progress."

The fact that these false approaches to faith—heteronomy and autonomy—are in bitter conflict is not surprising. When we understand what each is fighting against, we may even sympathize with their positions.

Representatives of the autonomous paradigm fight against the institutionalism and dogmatism of their opponents—rightfully so! Without doubt, in *this* battle I would like to be on their side. The same applies when we study what the heteronomists oppose: the spiritualism and irrationality of their opponents. They are correct in this battle as well.

The mistakes of both paradigms

So we can wholeheartedly agree with representatives of both sides—in view of what they oppose. Their (mutual) mistake is thinking that, when something is bad, the opposite of it must be necessarily good. But this is not the case. The only helpful alternative to both approaches is the bipolar thought model. As I demonstrate in the diagram to the right, neither the heteronomic nor the autonomous paradigms are even aware of the bipolar position in the middle. Heteronomists only see that, within the bipolar approach, institutions, doctrines and dogmas are not accepted as an end in themselves. This alone leads them to lump the theonomic paradigm together with the spiritualistic model of thinking.

The effects of the various paradigms on central theological issues.

In the same way, representatives of a spiritualistic approach to faith see that within the bipolar paradigm the institutional pole plays an important role. But since they are against institutions as a matter of principle, this information is enough for them to identify the theonomic and the heteronomic paradigms with each other.

In the diagram to the left I have tried to relate the three different approaches to faith (autonomy, heteronomy, and the bipolar paradigm) to various

Outcome of various paradigms
"Bipolar theology"

Danger to the left	Left pole	Right pole	Danger to the right
Autonomy	**Left pole**	**Right pole**	**Heteronomy**
Relativism	Faith	Doctrine	Dogmatism
Eclecticism	Word of God	Bibl. Canon	Fundamentalism
Libertinism	Love	Ethics	Legalism
Spiritualism	Fellowship	Sacraments	Sacramentalism
Docetism	Change	Tradition	Traditionalism
Separatism	Multiplication	Cooperation	Monopolism
Individualism	Spiritual gifts	Offices	Clericalism
Anarchism	Social service	Order	Conservatism
Quietism	Evangelism	Proclamation	Universalism

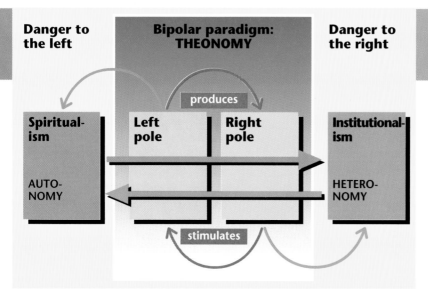

| Danger to the left | Bipolar paradigm: THEONOMY | Danger to the right |

Neither institution-alists nor spiritual-ists can think in a bipolar way. Instead of consid-ering the theo-nomic paradigm, they use their best energy battling against each other.

controversial issues which have been discussed throughout church history and are still being discussed today. Those who study these discussions more closely will notice with amazement that the same clichés are being promoted again and again, without any real com-munication taking place.

It can quite easily be shown that every individual debate is just a variation of the eternal battle of heteronomy against autonomy, in-stitutionalism against spiritualism, objectivism against subjectivism. The bipolar paradigm, which would solve problems in an astonish-ingly simple manner, is given no chance at all. These debates have been going on already for 2000 years without any significant progress. If a paradigm shift does not soon take place, we can be sure that battles of this nature will continue in the next millennium to rob the Christians of their best energy.

Communication is out of the question

The debate between the various paradigms is not at all a highly ab-stract issue which only concerns theologians. No, in the final analysis this structure is at the bottom line of most conflicts within our churches.

Basic structure of most conflicts

In the following chapter, I would like to illustrate this through two examples: first by explaining the different perceptions of a central Bible verse; second, by taking a short look at the conflict about spiri-tual gifts. These examples are just illustrations which could be supplemented by innumerable more. They are meant to show how much wrong theological thought patterns dominate literally all ar-eas of church life.

"Here we have two completely different approaches to faith in conflict with each other."

Different paradigms function like glasses: Representatives of the heteronomic paradigm read in Matthew 10:39 the command to self-denial, while representatives of the autonomous understanding of faith use the same verse as evidence for self-fulfillment.

Different paradigms function like glasses: I can look at the same facts, even at the same verses of Scripture, and yet see something completely different—depending on which glasses I am wearing.

Look for example at the words of Jesus which we find in Matthew 10:39: "Whoever finds his life will lose it; and whoever loses his life for my sake will find it." A typical example of the bipolar thought structure in the Bible, this verse speaks of losing one's life as well as finding it. Both correlate with each other (see diagram on the left below). Representatives of the heteronomic paradigm see—in this verse as well as in others—exclusively the word "lose," while representatives of the autonomous paradigm are only aware of the expressions about "finding." One can certainly not accuse both that their approaches are not "biblical" (both are referring to the Bible, and rightfully so!), but they have preconceived ideas, a filter—their glasses—through which only a partial aspect of the biblical message can penetrate.

Regardless to which issue we apply the competing thought patterns, the results can be easily predicted. Consider just the debate about spiritual gifts (see diagram on the right). Within the bipolar paradigm the following holds true: Every Christian has (at least) one spiritual gift. These gifts must be designated to certain offices or ministries. The offices, on the other hand, have to be useful—that is the only justification of their existence—so that the ministry of the different gifts can function effectively.

What does the subject look like from the perspective of the institutionalistic paradigm? Since the right pole is isolated from its left counterpart, the left pole is almost made unnecessary. Offices are considered as ends in themselves. They are not given to those persons who have the required spiritual gifts. The whole procedure is turned upside down. Through ordination the spiritual gifting—one at least believes—is automatically received. I have termed this approach clericalism. In the final analysis, this position

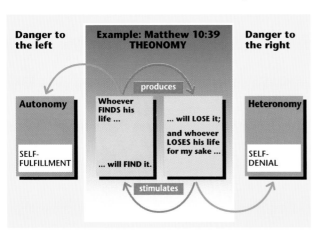

Danger to the left	Example: Matthew 10:39 THEONOMY	Danger to the right
Autonomy	Whoever FINDS his life ... — produces → ... will LOSE it; and whoever LOSES his life for my sake ...	Heteronomy
SELF-FULFILLMENT	... will FIND it. ← stimulates	SELF-DENIAL

makes the church body almost unnecessary. In this thought paradigm, the church *is* the pastor, the cleric. If "co-workers" are required at all, it is only as helpers for the pastor. It would be better if the pastor could carry out all the spiritual ministries alone, but since this is not possible, the "laity" must jump in to help solve the cleric's time problems.

The other extreme is the individualism of the spiritualistic paradigm. Individualism does not necessarily mean passivity. Some spiritualists can produce tremendous amounts of work. But since they refuse to relate their gifts to specific tasks in the church, their ministry is primarily done individually, in a direction determined by their own ego. Thus a coordination of gifts for church development is impossible—an approach which is also supported by the spiritualistic view that spiritual gifts are exclusively identifiable with the spontaneous, supernatural, and spectacular.

Why agreements are difficult to achieve

Some debates between charismatics and evangelicals reveal this basic difference. Sometimes it appears that these groups are arguing about whether or not three or four gifts mentioned in the New Testament have ceased to exist at the end of the Apostolic Age. If the discussion were really a question of this detail, then the vehemence of the battle would be hard to understand. No, we are dealing with much more. Here two completely different concepts of faith are in conflict with each other: heteronomy against autonomy, institutionalism against spiritualism, clericalism against individualism. Behind these positions are basically different images of God. This is the reason why we can make very little progress on this issue—as well as others—by getting involved in the arguments which are usually used in these debates. The problem is at another level: representatives of both opposing paradigms *cannot* understand each other. Neither biblical nor empirical arguments will be able to convince them to change their minds—unless a "paradigm shift" takes place.

Whereas in the bipolar paradigm, spiritual gifts and offices are connected with each other, they are isolated from each other by the extreme positions to the right (clericalism) and to the left (individualism).

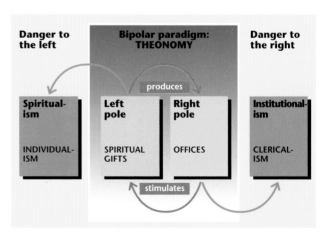

12 How Paradigms Change

"Reformation begins where the segmentation of God ceases."

In the diagram to the right I have tried to show how the different paradigms mentioned on the last pages are related to our different views of God. At the same time this diagram clarifies at which point alone a solution to the problem can be expected: by a movement toward the center. In other words: by developing a trinitarian experience of God.

But what can we do to promote that type of process? In my ministry, I have had good experiences with the following five guidelines.

Avoid manipulation

1. Never try to change another person's paradigm. Unlike some books which explain how to change people's mind in three or five or seven steps, I am basically skeptical of such efforts. Paradigm shifts cannot be forced or manipulated. The only paradigm which you can directly influence is your own.

Learn from your opponents

2. Try to learn from your opponents. Practice putting on the "glasses" of a different thought system, and you will understand other positions much better. Through my seminars, I have discovered that immense progress in this area can be made in just a weekend. Every person—no matter how syncretistic, dogmatistic, or spiritualistic he or she may be—has something to teach. Mind you, learning from others does not imply having to take over their whole system!

Create healthy feelings of insecurity

3. Create a climate where change can easily happen. Even if you cannot change the paradigms of other people, you can certainly do something: namely create a climate in which changes are more likely to happen. One of the best ways of doing this is using "alienation techniques," i.e. getting people to picture reality from a completely new perspective. This creates an insecurity which can be healthy and, in view of a paradigm shift, necessary. Work toward making the secure become insecure, the meaningless meaningful, and the reasonable unreasonable.

Welcome conflicts

4. Welcome conflicts between paradigms. Paradigm shifts happen almost exclusively through existential crises. Existing conflicts, if strong enough, can illicit such crises. If there are conflicts in your environment, do not complain about them, but consider these opportunities. Do not try to smooth them over with diplomatic formulas. Debates between representatives which are (in our trinitarian model) "outside the circle," can be dealt with in a way that will help both parties change their paradigms.

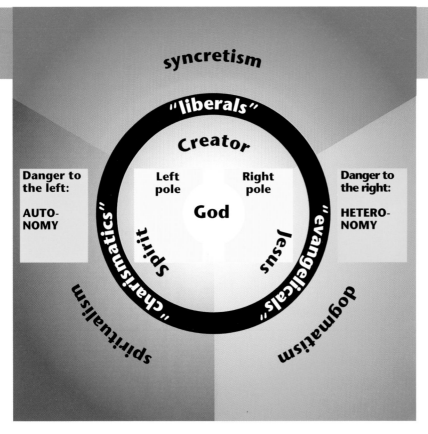

The diagram indicates how the bipolar paradigm is connected with our understanding of the Trinity. While dangers to the right and to the left are characterized by not being able to think in a bipolar way, the green segment includes a danger which is bipolar, but no longer Christian (syncretism).

Strengthen opposing poles

5. Instead of struggling against heresies, strengthen the opposing poles. No doubt all terms outside the black circle are referring to "heresies." How can we overcome them? The best way is to strengthen the respective opposing poles. In other words: Where light spreads, the darkness disappears all by itself. Does someone tend to syncretism? Then strengthen the red and blue element. Does someone tend toward dogmatism or spiritualism? Then it would be good for this person to especially focus on the green sector. In reality the opposite procedure is usually followed: evangelicals fight, above all, against syncretism and spiritualism (instead of letting go of dogmatism), liberals fight against spiritualism and dogmatism (instead of seeing their real danger, namely syncretism), etc.

What causes change?

From people concerned with change processes, church development, and revival, I frequently hear, "Christian, teaching principles, as you do, will change nothing. What we need is the anointing by the Holy Spirit." Others say, "All these charismatic meetings don't achieve anything. What people need is clear analytical thinking." Still others say, "If Jesus is not our motivation, then the best techniques and the most beautiful emotional experiences do not do a thing."

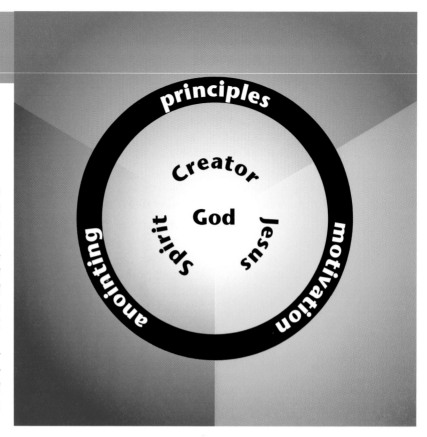

Those who have understood the principles (green segment), are not automatically motivated (red segment) and anointed (blue segment) to put them into practice. Vice versa: Neither motivation nor anointing should replace dealing with the principles.

Principles plus motivation plus anointing = reformation

Who is right? The diagram above shows that each of these three judgements is, in a way, right—and at the same time false. The truth is that we desperately need all three aspects. We learn the principles from the green segment—but thereby we are not motivated or anointed to practice them. On the other hand, all experiences of motivation (red segment) and anointing (blue segment) lead us no further, if we do not keep to God's principles of creation. But wherever all three dimensions come together, we can expect fundamental change.

Principles plus *motivation* plus *anointing*—that is a combination which could release explosive power! Real reformation takes place whenever the segmentation of God ceases, where Christians come together, where our experience of God becomes whole.

Epilogue

My goal in writing this booklet has not been to answer all of your questions or to solve all of your problems. That is something you have to do yourself. In fact, after reading this booklet, new questions may even have arisen. My goal is to bring *new light* to the questions that you are dealing with, both in your church and in your personal life.

What can you do with this booklet? Depending on your situation, some of the four following suggestions may help you:

1. You can relate the content to your own spiritual life and ask yourself: Where am I, at the moment, in my personal relationship to God? If you relate most strongly to one of the three segments, then you should ask yourself: At what point am I in danger? What could I do to overcome this danger? To which segment should I devote my attention in order to experience more growth in my relationship to God? **Determine your spiritual position**

2. This booklet can serve as an instrument to better understand the existing conflicts on a local, regional, and interdenominational level. I am well aware that an analysis alone cannot resolve any conflict. But I have learned through experience that it can be the first step toward a solution if we relate the paradigms as described in this booklet to complicated conflicts. **Understand conflicts**

3. If you have already begun to apply the principles of natural church development to your own church life, this booklet will help you to better understand the opposition you inevitably will encounter—and hopefully it will enable you to deal with this opposition in a more constructive way. **Develop churches naturally**

4. Finally, as I have written this booklet I have thought of the readers of my book *Paradigm Shift in the Church* who would like to share the concepts in that book with others, but who do not consider a theological textbook of about 300 pages very suitable for this purpose. I am well aware that we could not cover every important aspect on these 32 pages—but if we tried to touch on all of them, this booklet would lose its character as a *first introduction* to a new theological paradigm. **Promote paradigm shifts**

Whatever your position is, I would like to convince you of one thing: the question of the Trinity is not an ivory-tower fringe issue. It has to do with the center of theology, the center of the Christian faith, and the center of church life. Most importantly, how does it impact your life?

From the same author

Paradigm Shift in the Church

Paradigm Shift in the Church is the main theological work of Christian A. Schwarz. In this book he explains in context the theological premises behind natural church development. Opposition against church growth, with which every Christian leader has to deal, suddenly appears in a completely new light.

280 pages/hardback
Retail $19.95

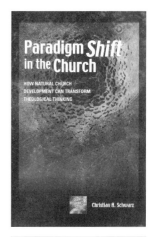

Natural Church Development

Here the author presents a new approach to church development: instead of trying to "make" church growth happen, he emphasizes the release of growth automatisms by which God himself grows his church. This book has been published in about 30 languages.

128 pages/four color/hardback
Retail $19.95

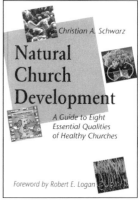

Implementation Guide to Natural Church Development

This book guides a church through the process of developing a strategy to address the minimum factors discovered through taking the Natural Church Development Survey.

235 pages/paperback
Retail $14.95

ChurchSmart Resources, 350 Randy Road – Suite 5, Carol Stream, IL 60188, USA
Phone: 1-800-253-4276 or (++1) 630-871-2598 • Fax: (++1) 630.871.8708
E-mail: Churchsmart@compuserve.com